Bouncing Back From Church Hurt

By

Dr. Kenton Edward Emmanuel Connor

TABLE OF CONTENT

INTRODUCTION

Regarding discipline and forgiveness within the church, Jesus said:

"If another member of the church sins against you, go and point out the fault when the two of you are alone... "
~Matthew 18:15a

Because the church is a spiritual hospital, many are the maimed, diseased, and partially paralysed - indeed, all of us have our broken bits to contend with and, therefore, necessarily, others must contend also. Others must put up with us, as we must put up with others. And such is the testament of love that, largely, we achieve this in the gladness and degrees of humour.

But inevitably things run awry.

Through lack of care/feedback/acknowledgement or criticism, church members are easily disenfranchised. Sometimes the people on the other end of the lack of care, feedback, or acknowledgement (etc) simply do not know their 'failing'. At other times they do, and issues prove irreconcilable.

PROBLEMS FOR THE HURT PERSON

What generally underpins the hurt within the person hurt is a history of hurt.

In such hurt is a history of unreconciled pain.

If we were to trace back through the passage of life of the person hurt we might expect to find significant irreconcilable issues, even quite disconnected from the present hurt. In this way, it is not just the presenting hurt that is the problem, but matters underneath compounding the present hurt.

It is a very unfortunate reality that, if, we suffered abuse and neglect as a child, we will be more susceptible to the ugliness of betrayal through our ensuing life. But the person who has grappled with such a disastrously broken past will not be so prone.

Unreconciled hurts build upon one another, to the point that incoming hurts cannot be handled at all well.

The best policy is rigorous honesty with ourselves, but the irony is the more hurt we are underneath the less desire we have to be honest. We may need honesty all the more, but we may have less

capacity than we need. As soon as we are honest we can understand that conflict needs to be addressed, so the situation, and ourselves, can be healed. This, of course, takes significant portions of courage.

THE CHALLENGE FOR THE HURT PERSON

Healing is a challenge for the hurt person. They may very well feel it is beyond them.

Healing rests in peace. Whatever outcome we seek we must be able to live with. When we are honest, and we accept that addressing the issue means confronting another person or people in love, we have a way of moving forward. But we need to be ready for both positive and negative results. We need to do this in order to protect ourselves.

Meeting the person one-on-one, having planned what we will say, and having prepared ourselves to listen to them also, we communicate clearly and concisely. We harness our emotions by keeping mindful of how they might be feeling.

Whatever happens, the challenge for the person who has been hurt is to meet the perpetrator of the hurt, wherever possible, and seek an acceptable reconciliation.

If such an acceptable reconciliation isn't possible, the hurt person is presented with a challenge not too uni□ue in this life - to accept the things they cannot change, in the knowledge that they did the best they could.

***

Church hurts are an ever present threat. When they occur we cannot let them fester. Jesus has commanded us to meet the person who has hurt us. This is the way we move forward. Having done this, we either addressed the hurt through courage or we learned to accept that which we could not change. Either way we can have peace and, therefore, healing.

Situations of hurt need to be resolved through actions of reconciliation; a process by which the hurt person needs to initiate.

CHURCH HURT - RELIGION OR RELATIONSHIP?

Church - a place of sanctity and solace - a safe haven - a place where you can find rest for your "weary soul" -a shelter from the storms of life. I have heard it referred to as a "hospital" -- a place where the wounded can find a "balm in Gilead"; where the broken hearted can be mended; where the lame can "take up their beds and walk"; where blinded eyes can be opened, and deaf ears can be unstopped. Church - a refugee camp - a place for the outcast - the derelict - a "home for the homeless", "life for the lifeless", "hope for the hopeless", you know those who are rejected, neglected, and ejected by the world and its pandemonium. Church - a holistic place-a place of restoration and wholeness-- where those who are hemorrhaging; who have had an "issue of blood" for many years-unbearable pain and suffering-- going from doctor-to-doctor and psychiatry-to-psychiatry; who have exhausted all resources-penniless--broke--in despair--searching for just one touch-- seeking to be made whole again! But what happens when the very place that you turn to when you are hurting...hurts you? What happens when those who have been commissioned and ordained to "put Humpty-Dumpty back together again" are the ones who

caused Humpty to "have a great fall"? I am sure if I conducted a survey and sent it out to 1000 church goers, I would find that at least half of them have experienced "Church Hurt".

Over twenty years ago, I wrote a play entitled, "The Light", based on the biblical account of the "good Samaritan, which depicts a well-renown Bishop, who is invited as a guest speaker to a small town church's "annual Christmas revival". The members of the church had heard of him and how he had performed many miracles; yet they had never seen or met him face-to-face. On the bishop's arrival into this small town, while walking down the street, he is mugged by two local thugs. A short while later, a group of church leaders passed by, whom he asked for assistance, but they refused. As I stated earlier, the very ones who were commissioned and ordained to help him were the ones who "snubbed up" their noses at him. However he encountered a runaway teenager-who fed him; a bag lady-who sung him a song of comfort; and a homeless man-who offered him a sleeping bag to rest for the night. Sometimes love and compassion are shown through those in which we least expect and "gifts" comes in small packages. Well, the Bible tells us not to despise "small" beginnings (that is just an extra tidbit for someone who needed it).

Nevertheless, "Church Hurt"-hurts like no other hurt; it is more intense. The thing about "Church Hurt", you never know when it is coming or who it is coming from-it could be a choir member, an auxiliary leader, an usher, the church mother, the pastor's wife, or even the pastor. Now, you talk about hurt-when your pastor hurt you-that is some severe hurt. It is a gut-wrenching blow that knocks all of the wind out of your sail. Nevertheless, it is a reality; it happens! Stephanie Mills sung a song a few years ago entitled, "I Never Knew Love Like This Before!" I could do a remake entitled, "I Never Knew Pain Like This Before!" But she also states in the song, "Open My Eyes" "Church Hurt" does just that "Open Your Eyes!" You will realize that the only thing in this world that you can depend on is the unadulterated (pure) Word of God! People will fail you, but the Word of God NEVER fails. Before I move on to my next point, I must leave a warning to the shepherds who impose "Church Hurt" found in Ezekiel 34:4 and 34:10:

4) The diseased have ye not strengthened, neither have ye healed that which was sick, neither have ye bound up that which was broken, neither have ye brought again that which was driven away, neither have ye sought that which was lost; but with force and with cruelty have ye ruled them.

10) This is what the Sovereign LORD says: I am against the shepherds and will hold them accountable for my flock. I will remove them from tending the flock so that the shepherds can no longer feed themselves. I will rescue my flock from their mouths, and it will no longer be food for them.

Now, let's talk about how we position ourselves to get hurt. Some of us were raised in church and became quite familiar with the traditionalism of going to church because it was the "right" thing to do! Some of us attended church because there was a need or point of lack in our lives! And some of us attended church because we were broken, busted, and disgusted and were seeking a balm or some type of solace. The common denominator that linked all these scenarios is the Pastor. At our original entrance in the church, we may have needed instructions, guidance, or a roadmap to get back on our feet or to steer us in the right way, because we did not know "The Way" (Jesus is The Way, The Truth, and The Life [John 14:6]). However, once we get on our feet and become acquainted with "The Way", we no longer need our "crutch". What I am trying to say that some of us become co-dependent on man (the Pastor and the Church body), instead of solely depending on and putting our trust in "The Way". First, let me say that Pastors should be reverenced, given

honor, and esteemed-highly. But there is a thin line between "reverenced" and "idolized". There is a distinction between "honored" and "put on a pedestal". There is a contrast between "esteemed-highly " and "worshipped". Besides, our God is a jealous God; He will not have any other god before him (See Exodus 34:14). Is it possible that He imposes measures to break "the apron strings" of dependency that you have placed before him? Is it possible that He allows situations to occur that "open our eyes" ? Just maybe that measure could very well be "Church Hurt". Once we are free from the addiction of man-we can now fully and wholeheartedly receive the anointing of God; who will teach us all things.

1 John 2:27: But the anointing which ye have received of him abideth in you, and ye need not that any man teach you: but as the same anointing teacheth you of all things, and is truth, and is no lie, and even as it hath taught you, ye shall abide in him.

Let me clarify, I am not advocating emancipation, or separation from the church, nor am I telling anyone not to listen to their Pastor, so let us get that straight right now. I am a minister and I certainly would not do anything to disrespect my ministerial calling or for that matter, those who have been called to Pastor. But what I am saying

to you is what a Pastor told me several years ago that changed my life, "Get to know God for yourself." Do not let your relationship with God solely be determined by a 15-30 minute sermon. Study the Word of God for yourself. 2 Timothy 2:15 confirms, "Study to show thyself approved, a workman that needed not be ashamed, rightly dividing the word of truth." Read your Bible! If you have trouble understanding the Word, by all means seek for understanding from a clergy or someone who is an astute student of the Word.

In conclusion, I have certainly had my share of "Church Hurt" but it has only strengthened me; for my trials have only made me stronger, wiser, and better. "Church Hurt" has made me re-focus my priorities and place my trust in the Lord (Proverbs 3). It has taught me that I do not have to be a "clone" of someone else; that I can uniquely and individually be "me". It has made me live the advice of my Pastor, the late Georgia Smith, "Get to know God for yourself!" Each day I am learning more..! Experience a "relationship" not a "religion-ship". You will be glad you did!

THE UNHEALTHY BODY OF CHRIST

The church has become sick because some of the people in it are infected. I know because I was one of them. I believe that God is calling for order in His church. In order for the body of Christ to become healthy there must be order. I served in a leadership role, and also as the youth pastor, before my illness was diagnosed. It wasn't until the Dr.'s (my Bishop and Pastor), took away my title and sat me down, that I began to notice how infected I was. You see, the church only becomes sick and infected when the leaders of the church turn their heads and just put Band-Aids on the infected areas. Some of the infections in the body of Christ are Rebellion, Disobedience, and not following proper Protocol, to name a few.

I know these exist, for I myself, have operated in all of them. It's because of this experience that God has shown me the prescription for these infections. I guess before I begin to talk about the prescriptions, I need to explain how I got infected. It all began with being deceived, which opened the door to everything else. I've found that deception begins with thoughts. Every time I agreed with the enemy, I was empowering him to act.

Thoughts that have good motives, but incorrect timing, cause us to follow our opinions. The voice of the enemy is very subtle. He's saying and confirming what you already know, then we fall into error and move out of the timing of God. Familiar spirits know us very well and deceive us by what we are attracted to, by putting our gifts before God and by having us substitute position and power - for God's presence.

So here I was the youth pastor and everything was going great, until I was called into the office. At that time, the "Holy Spirit" spoke for me and all I could hear in my spirit was the word (exposed). Let me explain, you see I was giving permission to have a bible study, outside of my church. I was given specific instructions on how it should operate. First, let me tell you that I didn't get this approval until after I had already had everything in place. This was the first mistake. I was told to have it only once a month and I had it twice a month. I was told no retreats and I had retreats etc., you get the picture. I felt that there was no harm in doing what God had called me to do, so I continued operating in disobedience, which led to rebellion, completely out of order.

I also found that I wasn't alone in this area and that many people in the body of Christ have a deaf ear when it comes to order. The congregations

have been unconsciously running the churches by their opinions and how they see things. Every thought/comment that is contradicting to what the direction/vision of the leader is, releases a sabotage spirit.

Sabotage - an action taken to undermine or destroy somebody's efforts or achievements

We seem to find people who are in agreement with how we feel. We won't go to the office and get a clear understanding for ourselves; instead we have sheep counseling sheep, blind leading the blind. All while, the enemy is watching us sabotage the vision. It's the silent killer of our church. If we are to be connected to our churches, we must be connected to the leaders.

Many Bishops and Pastors may not have taken the stand that my leaders did. It could be simply because they don't want to hurt people's feelings or maybe the person is a great tithe payer, so they really don't want to upset them. Or maybe, they don't want the person to leave the church therefore ruining the leader's reputation. Whatever their reasoning are, I have to thank God for my leaders, who listened to the direction of God, put me on bed rest (sat me down), and wasn't concerned what it looked like.

1 Thessalonians 5:12-13 - The Message (MSG) 12-13 And now, friends, we ask you to honor those leaders who work so hard for you, who have been given the responsibility of urging and guiding you along in your obedience. Overwhelm them with appreciation and love!

By them taking this stand, I experience complete humiliation, heartache and hurt. I truly felt that this was the 'death of me.' Nevertheless, in spite of the gossip and the effect this had on myself and family, I forced myself to go the church and sit on the front row (which was the instructions (prescription) I was given). From the messages that were being delivered, I was able to start my healing process. God showed me so many areas in my life that were not pleasing to Him and truly infected. He was performing surgery and removing everything that was not like Him. Little by little restoration began. I was being transformed from the inside out. My life has never been the same! After some time, I realized that It's wasn't what my leaders had done to me... but rather what they did for me.

I truly believe that the body of Christ will begin to heal, when the leaders administer the prescription of correction. They work under strict supervision of God.

Hebrews 13:17-The Message (MSG)-17 Be responsive to your pastoral leaders. Listen to their counsel. They are alert to the condition of your lives and work under the strict supervision of God. Contribute to the joy of their leadership, not its drudgery. Why would you want to make things harder for them?

What we must realize is that God uses our leaders and has placed them in authority over us. So if you find yourself, as I did, being corrected, make sure that you are obedient to the voice of God. Don't be so quick to leave your church. I wanted to leave, but God said "no". Don't be influenced by others, because only you know what God is telling you.

Hebrews 12:5-11 The Message (MSG)- 4-11 In this all-out match against sin, others have suffered far worse than you, to say nothing of what Jesus went through-all that bloodshed! So don't feel sorry for yourselves. Or have you forgotten how good parents treat children, and that God regards you as his children?

My dear child, don't shrug off God's discipline, but don't be crushed by it either.

It's the child he loves that he disciplines; the child he embraces, he also corrects.

God is educating you; that's why you must never drop out. He's treating you as dear children. This trouble you're in isn't punishment; it's training, the normal experience of children. Only irresponsible parents leave children to fend for themselves. Would you prefer an irresponsible God? We respect our own parents for training and not spoiling us, so why not embrace God's training so we can truly live? While we were children, our parents did what seemed best to them. But God is doing what is best for us, training us to live God's holy best. At the time, discipline isn't much fun. It always feels like it's going against the grain. Later, of course, it pays off handsomely, for it's the well-trained who find themselves mature in their relationship with God.

Leaders have a responsibility to set order and correct. God is calling for a healthy church.

WHICH CHURCH ARE YOU?

Before the Apostle John was taken in the Spirit to record the future events of the Revelation, he was instructed to record our Lord's first and only personal address to the Church (Revelation, Chapters 2 & 3): seven separate letters to seven specific churches that existed during John's day.

- Ephesus
- Smyrna
- Pergamos
- Thyatira
- Sardis
- Philadelphia
- Laodicea

These were real churches with real issues and Jesus responded to an actual condition particular to that congregation; sometimes commendatory, sometimes critical; but adapted perfectly to the particular situation He discovered in each.

But they were not random selections. Jesus specifically addressed these seven churches because each had a condition representative of the church as a whole in all ages and continue to exist in all churches today. Their problems are our problems. The Lord therefore still speaks with a

message as relevant for our churches and for each of us today as it was to those in the first century.

Jesus concludes each letter with a warning to the individual: "He who has an ear, let him hear what the Spirit says to the churches." May we hear and heed what Christ, through the Spirit, says to us personally concerning these matters.

EPHESUS (2:1-7)

"Insincere"

Jesus applauds the works of the Ephesians. They labored hard to serve the church, persevered in their duties with patience, didn't tolerate evil members, rejected false teachers and doctrines, and they did it gladly for His name's sake without growing weary. "Nevertheless I have this against you, that you have left your first love."

Our Lord's issue with Ephesus was clearly not the quantity or the quality of their works, for He emphasizes both a zeal and steadfastness. Instead, Jesus was identifying a departure from their earlier "first love". Though this is not explained, because love for God and love for one another are the two greatest commandments, allow me to speculate what might have been happening.

Rather than a passionate desire to worship God as it was in the beginning, church attendance became an obligation or force of habit; and fellowship, once a fervent love for one another, became argumentative and divisive. In other words, that early love where we denied self, gladly abandoned all that displeases God, and joyfully embraced fellowship one with another had waned in Ephesus and the members were simply "going through the motions without emotion."

In response, Jesus calls the Ephesians to remember, repent, and return to the place from where they had fallen otherwise He would remove their "lampstand" from its place and essentially put it "on the shelf". That is, He would disqualify their service as a light-bearer to uphold and illuminate Him to the world and would no longer effectively use them for opportunities to shine the light of the gospel unto others.

As Christians, we are the light of the world; vessels empowered by the Holy Spirit to enlighten hearts with the true love and glory of God in His Son, Jesus Christ. When our hearts no longer abound in love, however, we quench the work of the Spirit and thereby render our witness and testimony inadequate to serve as a lamp to uphold Jesus, who is the light. May our worship,

works and fellowship always flow from a pure heart genuinely in love with Jesus that we may present ourselves as a vessel sanctified and useful for God to proclaim His great love to those dwelling in darkness.

SMYRNA (2:8-11)

"Suffering"

The church at Smyrna is the Lord's choice to illustrate the suffering church and its needs. As such, their message is one of comfort and the first of only two churches in these letters Jesus has only praise for.

Smyrna was under severe persecution from a malignant group of Jews that Jesus calls blasphemous members of the "synagogue of "Satan"-vile men falsely claiming to be Jews spiritually who were being used as instruments of the devil to vehemently oppose Christ and His Church.

Christians suffer persecution because the world hates God. Some are light afflictions like ridicule, false accusations, scorn, or perhaps the loss of friendships, while others are heavier afflictions of imprisonment and death such as our dear brothers and sisters in other parts of the world are

enduring. God alone knows why the disparity. But the Sufferer surrounds all His suffering ones and none of us ever passes through any trial of unjust persecution or worldly contempt that He has not known, overcome, and has promised to see us through.

In response, Jesus calls for the members to not be afraid but to remain faithful throughout the affliction and torment and death. That by their patient endurance they would pass through the trials as He did and thereafter be rewarded with a crown of life and an everlasting joy in the world to come; never again to be hurt by the first death, or empowered by the second death.

As Christians, we will suffer in this life when we desire to live godly for Jesus because it has been granted on behalf of Christ, not only to believe in Him, but also to suffer for His sake. This seems strange because suffering is difficult. But our afflictions for Christ are gifts from God working for us a far more exceeding and internal weight of glory: the promise of joy unspeakable when His glory is revealed. Still, we never suffer alone. Our risen Lord stands with us and His Spirit covers us with sufficient grace. May we follow Jesus through suffering with patience, knowing God has appointed it for our blessing in anticipation of the

eternal hope of glory He has laid up for us in heaven.

PERGAMOS (2:12-17)

"Compromising"

Jesus commends the church for holding fast to His name and maintaining a true faith in Him all the while surrounded by temples and shrines and innumerable idols in the darkest center of pagan abominations He refers to as "Satan's seat."

As with Ephesus, the issue Jesus had with Pergamos was not about their lack of steadfastness to His name. Jesus rebukes the congregation for permitting ungodly men with carnal doctrines into the church. Seemingly Pergamos had not yet embraced their teachings, but by harboring and giving a seat to these false teachers they allowed a spirit of compromise with evil and seductive practices taught by the world to infiltrate the church.

In response, Jesus calls for the congregation to repent for allowing false teachers to freely coexist in the church and influence other members into accepting their pagan practices. "Repent, or else I will come to you quickly and will fight against them with the sword of my mouth." How this

intervention would play out is uncertain, but the prospect of our Lord fighting members in the congregation with the same verbal sword which one day He will smite the nations should strike fear in the church.

The issue for Pergamos was thinking that the church has the authority to decide what is right or wrong rather than identifying with the person of Jesus Christ and recognizing that He has given us the Word of God through the Holy Spirit as our only authority. In other words, the congregation blindly permitted the presence of heretics based upon church allowances rather than searching the Scriptures themselves to "test the spirits" whether they were of God.

As Christians, we're warned that many false prophets are in the world. We must therefore test every doctrine by the doctrinal truth taught by the Holy Spirit in the Word of God to expose beliefs taught by the spirit of this world. In fact, we're guilty of compromise when we say nothing even though we aren't practicing such things. We are the salt of the earth. May we always do the work of an evangelist when confronted by worldly philosophies and use the opportunity to preach the Word to convince, rebuke, and exhort with longsuffering and teaching those deceived by the

lie, that in hearing they might believe the truth and be saved.

THYATIRA (2:18-29)

"Apostate"

Our Lord gives honorable mention of the works, charity, faith and patience in Thyatira, even emphasizing that their latter works had grown more impressive than their earlier works. Still, the congregation was far from a right relationship with the Son of God and is sternly rebuked.

Thyatira was found guilty of entrusting an evil and bewitching "prophetess" named Jezebel to influence and teach the congregation into mingling pagan practices and idolatry with Christian works and worship as if she had supernatural revelation and divine approval to impose it.

As such, Thyatira represents the apostate church evolved. It not only enabled a false system of heresy entrance into the church as did Pergamos, but exalted it by granting "that woman Jezebel" authority to publicly introduce and beguile the congregation with her ungodly pagan rituals, idols, ceremonies and traditions.

Whether Jesus was identifying this woman by her actual name or merely pin-pointing a particular female member of the congregation who had been corrupting the church in the manner of the abominable ancient Queen Jezebel is unclear. Nonetheless some evil woman representative of a diabolical system did exist in Thyatira and is still very much influencing the Church today.

In response, Jesus levies a strong admonition of sickness against her and great tribulation and death against those unrepentant members who became converts and commit adultery with her. To those not holding to her doctrine He commands to hold fast with a cautionary warning not to let others wrest the truth away from them.

As Christians, we are unique because we proclaim one God, one Lord and Savior, Jesus Christ, and only one inspired revelation of God, the Bible. The world exalts diversity of belief and is content for everybody to have his own religious beliefs as if they all had equal merit-but Christianity is contrary to all of that! Christianity absolutely does not permit any part of the traditions, ceremonies, rituals or doctrines of any religious system to be mixed or mingled into it. Jesus is more than the man of history other religions acknowledge. He claimed to be God, was put to death for this claim,

and His resurrection substantiated this claim. May we always rightly divide the word of truth to expose and openly reject any clergy, priest, theologian or religious organization that preaches any other gospel regardless how righteous and holy they appear.

SARDIS (3:1-6)

"Spiritually Dead"

The Sardis letter contains no approval of good works or condemnation for blatant wickedness, only a searing admonition that all the while they outwardly appeared as a church alive in Christ, inwardly there was no life; they were dead and in dire need of the quickening power of the Holy Spirit.

Seemingly Sardis had once been known as a strong, Christ-honoring church, so they still had a name as a church in Christ, a pastoral leadership, and evidently most members were "professing" Christians. But other than using His name and conducting church, they denied the realities of the doctrine of salvation and were not reborn of the Spirit. The sad truth is that they were unsaved members just going through the motions of pseudo-Christianity unaware they had not passed from death to life.

In response, Jesus calls upon the unsaved members to repent because they would not be found blameless at His Coming. To the few genuine believers who were truly saved, He calls worthy of eternal life.

Salvation is a gift of God by grace through faith, not the result of our good works or good behavior or our membership in a church. We must be born again. We must admit that we're sinners willing to turn away from sin, believe that Jesus Christ died on the cross and resurrected again to achieve our salvation, and then ask Him to become our Lord and Savior. As we do, we are instantly "born again" from above and given a new nature and a new heart and a spiritual life sealed by the indwelling of His Spirit for the day of redemption. There is no other way; this is where eternal life begins.

As Christians, we became new creatures in Christ entirely different from what we were before by our new birth. We were spiritually reborn as a child of God into His family and by His Spirit God now lives within us. May we always be influenced and empowered to walk and live and be led by the Holy Spirit, for it is His Spirit that God has given us and to everyone that believeth.

PHILADELPHIA (3:7-13)

"Faithful"

This church was maintaining a faithful witness in the midst of general apostasy and unbelief and is commended for keeping the Word of the Lord and not denying His name and the letter is without any rebuke or suggestion of judgment.

Philadelphia was not found guilty of the sins practiced in Ephesus, Pergamos, Thyatira and Sardis. Their love was sincere, they tested the spirits to keep out false teachers, rightly divided the word to prevent mixing worldly philosophies with the true gospel, and they were born-again by the Holy Spirit. As such, they represent the persevering, spiritually awakened and faithful church that keeps His word and does not deny His deity or His completed work on the cross.

In response, Jesus promises to set before them an "open door, and no man can shut it", and to keep them from "the hour of trial, which shall come upon the whole world, to test them that dwell

upon the earth." Both promises apply to the church as a whole in what I deem to be a significant way.

Our Lord's first assurance is that He has set before it an "open door" to preach the gospel throughout the world as an instrument for salvation despite any attempt to prevent it. This, of course, has been the case for the Church from the beginning and explains why it has survived two thousand years of adversity and opposition and continues to spread the gospel throughout the world today.

The second is somewhat more controversial but I believe is one of the key verses supporting the doctrine of the rapture of the believing church. The "hour of trial which shall come upon the whole earth" refers to the future tribulation described by the prophets as seven years of calamity, chaos and judgment poured from the vials of God's wrath unlike anything the world or man has ever experienced. This is a time of vengeful judgment. But given our Lord's assurance to deliver Philadelphia from this coming hour, we must therefore conclude that genuine believers will be delivered by Christ Himself before the appointed wrath as He returns to take them by resurrection and rapture to be with Him.

As Christians, we're deserving of nothing and yet have been given exceedingly great and precious promises. Let us remain steadfast to keep His Word and with patience and perseverance hold fast to the crown given us for our work of faith, labor of love, and patience of hope in our Lord Jesus Christ. We can be comforted to know that we may be caught up at any moment to meet the Lord in the air for Jesus says, "Behold, I come quickly!" Let us therefore watch and be sober that we need not be ashamed at His appearance. Let us be confident we have fought the good fight so we can boldly respond without any uncertainty, "Amen. Even so, come, Lord Jesus!"

LAODICEA (3:14-22)

"Lukewarm"

This is a strong rebuke against a church that allowed their wealth and financial well-being to blind them to the reality of their own spiritual depravity and contains no Godly praise or the mentioning of any good works and no indication that any member was above approach.

The issue for Laodicea was that they allowed worldly possessions and fascinations to dilute their burning desire for the Lord Jesus Christ

until they became spiritually lukewarm-neither hot nor cold-neither fervent for God, nor bitterly opposed to God. But they had drifted so far away from an intimacy with God that they lacked the spiritual compass to recognize it. In their own worldly eyes they felt no need to change things because they were comfortable just as they were.

In response, Jesus calls for them to "wake up and see" the truth about the wretched and miserable state they were in because their condition was repugnant to Him and would lead to chastening. "I am about to spew you out of My mouth." And yet, upon a church whose hearts had shut Jesus out, the risen Lord still yearns to restore fellowship with them. "Behold, I stand at the door, and knock."

Unlike Sardis whom Jesus warned of judgment because they had not attained salvation, this is a plea from our heavenly Father to a "prodigal son" whom He loves and continues to pursue, but also will rebuke and discipline as a son in order to uncover and correct the problem. God alone knows what manner of chastening, but at the very least I believe they would no longer be partakers of the abundant life and fullness of joy promised to those who abide in Him, and He in them-at the very least they would lose the joy of their salvation and live sad spiritually unfulfilled lives.

As Christians, our fervent desire to know and draw closer to God more intimately can quickly cool by any circumstance that provides a sense of contentment. Wealth and prosperity, certainly, because money supplies material things without a need to call upon God; and over time, by devoting less time in prayer and supplication before God we simply connect with Him less. The issue however isn't a satisfactory life style, for contentment with godliness is great gain because it's finding joy in what God has given to us. The issue is when we take God out of the equation: feeling enriched enough with ourselves to devote less time in prayer and worship, reading the Word, exercising our spiritual gifts, and fellowshipping with the saints. This is the danger zone-when we become satisfied spending less time with God rather than thirsting for more-this is what summons our Lord to beckon and discipline if necessary. May we continue earnestly praying for God to search our hearts and minds so He can reveal any wicked way in us that requires correction. He loved us so much that He gave His only begotten Son that we may have life and that eternally. How can we not but love Him with all our heart and with all our soul and with all our mind and strength?

"Now the God of peace, who brought up from the dead the great Shepherd of the sheep through the blood of the eternal covenant, even Jesus our Lord, equip you in every good thing to do His will, working in us that which is pleasing in His sight, through Jesus Christ, to whom be the glory forever and ever. Amen" - Hebrews 13:20-21

THINKING, BEHAVIOR, RELIGION AND CHURCH

Thinking and behavior, in the name of religion and church, seem foul sometimes. Instead of avoiding or blaming, a little experiment can be done. Religion and church can be evaluated to determine if they really are the source of thinking and behavior. This effort has to be scientific, minus the human emotionalism quite often attending the subjects of religion or church. The research will also be metaphysical, indicative to the evidence that thought and behavior is infinite, yet never idle.

It is not an arguing point in this experiment to say human beings are connected to, or disconnected from, religion and church. Religion and church are associated with systems of beliefs. Basically, we all do have a system of beliefs. Scientists, clergy, physicians, sports fans, aid-workers, the strange neighbor, and so on do not only believe something, but also act on those beliefs religiously. Admittedly, belief systems are mind boggling. However, confusion diminishes as beliefs are broken down into simple components. A belief of love versus a belief in hate. A belief in principle versus a belief in randomness. Although

these simple components are almost too simple, simplicity is a valid starting point in research.

Love and Principle is the source of constructive, practical, healing, compassionate ideas and thus action. Religion or church did not invent or initiate Love, Principle. Although, religion and church can be tools by which enlightened understanding and behavior are brought to our attention; research reveals that systems of beliefs have no innate lasting power to create, authorize, or discredit, the thoughts and behavior of people. Ironically, belief systems that lack this knowledge will think human philosophies, agendas, and rituals, empower thinking and behavior. However, unnumbered people have acted on a particular belief for years until one day they realized the belief was bogus, easily changed by newly presented facts or by simply taking a stand for a better thought.

Believing in an ultimate love and principle is better than believing in an unbeatable hate and chaos. A love belief contributes to the positive nature of thinking and action, contributes to our humaneness. But love without principle, flusters. Principle has order and includes an understanding of what love really is; a love that disallows suffocation or hurt feelings. Because religion and church are not the source of thought

and behavior, they cannot be the source of humanities advancement. Also, they cannot be a source of foul play. Therefore, it would be backward either to love or hate religion and church. It is better to love Love and hate hate.

If human beings believe religion or church originates (or crushes) advancement they acquiesce to rote thoughts, creating unapproachable or callous behavior worthless to the well-being of people and our world. Effort put into comprehending Love, Principle, is necessary. Because to just believe what first pops into our heads concerning the truth of these topics, is not productive. Mary Baker Eddy wrote in Science and Health, "To seek Truth through belief in a human doctrine is not to understand the infinite." The infinite nature of Love, Principle, precludes the beliefs that advancement and inspired behavior can only come from a select group of people or at a particular time in human history. Someone, somewhere, now, is receiving a better concept of love and principle and applying it in their daily life. It is our right and responsibility to be aware of, and implement into every avenue of life, progressive ideas. If a small business owner in New Zealand decides to renovate her merchandise, making it more functional for the customers, we too can keep in mind how to better serve others.

It is essential to make sure we are not our own worst enemy to progressive beliefs. Decisions and choices are too often mechanically made based on our very limited mortal imprints and expectations. Meditation can help us disconnect from finite, even stubbornly ingrained beliefs. Prayer can allow us to reconnect with loving principled beliefs that yield to understanding. For example, years ago I believed any advancement in religion or church had to come from a religious or churchy person. But, just as genes mutate, my belief changed-improved. I discovered people who never went to church who were healing, who were serene, logical, powerful examples of the religion of Love. Conclusively, progress in healing and comfort exists. Perpetual advancement is not confined to a mortal or to the discoveries of mortals even if they call the discovery a religion or church.

I am not you, and you are not me. Religion is not church, and church is not religion. No one church has a monopoly on truth and no religion can be limited to a particular church. Understanding unites you and me, unites religion and church, but at no point does a church become religion or vice versa. Even if a religion and church seem to be born at the same time-like twins-they still are not one and the same. The true identities of religion

and church can't be distorted, discredited, or credited falsely, no matter how screwed up human belief systems and behavior can look. The object is to understand the Identities of Love, Principle, not so much the individualities of religion or church.

The individuality and unity of religion and church need to be viewed spiritually, with honesty and open-mindedness. If a belief system exaggeratedly magnifies the individuality of a religion or church, without appreciating the goodness of others, division is inevitable. Be aware though, if a belief system intensely strives to connect human beings, people mistakenly will assume that unity is to unify, to amalgamate into one and the same. Not possible. The Infinite is infinite uniqueness. Religions, churches, and human beings do not integrate into a similar, delineated body. Infinite identity requires endless unique individualities.

Religion and church are not the source of thought and behavior. They are thought and behavior. As effort is made to understand the thought and behavior of Love, Principle, instead of hate and uncertainty, religion and church can be seen as not something to avoid or blame but as something to include in our ever advancing world. Every effort made on the side of Love, Principle, will naturally diminish the tendency to repeat idle,

self-destructive belief systems. With an infinite, beliefs constantly improve and progress can be understood and experienced by us and our world.

IS YOUR CHURCH IN ALIGNMENT?

The Message driven Church

By message we are not talking about The Message, but the sub-message. The message of Jesus is usually always preached and does not change, but what about the sub-message or how the message is stated?

Is the sub-message, Jesus says... or how to fix a broken world... or help for hurting people? Does your church center around the Sunday service, is this where it happens?

The down side of a message driven Church is that is least likely to change and could be least flexible.

The up side of a message driven Church is that it is a strong voice as long as the person in charge is around, but may struggle when the leader dies or moves on.

The Medium driven Church

The medium driven Church could be a church with a strong Sunday School. It could be centered on the pulpit with one strong person. It could be the choir or a bus ministry. It could also be a TV ministry.

The up side is that it could be flexible or creative.

The down side is when it fixes in on one medium or one person.

The Market driven Church

The market driven Church is a church that aims for specific group or class of people, or any area that can be identified.

The up side is that it is usually the most creative and the most flexible. Always on top. Constant change.

The down side is that a market driven Church can become a slave to the market and with a highly market driven Church there is a high risk factor. Willing to comprise the message.

Good Alignment

When all three of these are in alignment with each other you have the best situation. They are all good, but they must have good alignment. They may not be in balance, but should be in alignment. For example the message must reach the market. To do this you must study and know your market. Who are you reaching for and who is available for you to reach.

How well do you communicate what you are to your church?
How well do you communicate what you are to your community?

Image is what others think you are.
Identity is what you know you are.

Try to merge image and identity so that others really know what you are all about.

Step One - Inspire commitment from your staff or board.
Step two - Develop a self-awareness.
Ask yourself what is the dominant theme for out church now? Use a five year maximum time frame.
What moments from my church's past and present are emblematic of our vision?
What do we want to say about our church and to whom?
If you try to appeal to everyone, you will not appeal to anyone.
Which truth about my church will I choose to represent us?
Pick only one and go forward with it. The one you pick is your identity and the one you go forward with is your image.

Marketing strategy
Be careful not to sell what you cannot deliver! You may not understand who you are.
Why do tag-lines matter? Think of it as your bumper sticker. It tells who you are and how you want to be seen.

A large southern church that has just come out of a long successful revival and is now trying to get

back to being a church again, has picked a tag-line (Explore Life Now). Their market is a large geographical area that the past revival reached and the congregation usually spends the weekend when coming to the church. With beaches nearby, the message is to come, attend church and enjoy the beaches.

A few bad tag-lines:
"It's not your father's Oldsmobile", Oldsmobile is no longer around, they drove off their older market by insulting the older drivers.

"Brown and Buddy", Pepsi Cola tag-line and it only ran one week. They were aiming for the black community and it drew all kinds of negative feedback.

A few good tag-lines:
"Just Do It" and "Where's The Beef?" This one lasted about 5 years in the 80's and was only dropped during the 90's due to weight becoming a public issue.

Look for a good advertisement company for your church, they will know how to make use of the subliminal messages in the selection of color fonts and graphics in your ads.

Avoid using real people from your congregation in your ads, you never know what may happen to them and you may have to pull an expensive ad.

If you ever blame a consumer, you have lost them. Blame is the result of negative guilt. Not all guilt is negative.

Remember that all non-profits require funding.

People will develop an image about ur church, but will it be what we want? Let's give them our image!

Orientation

What is the magnet north for your Church? If you shake a compass it will always return back to the same direction. What ever your church goes through, the direction it returns to is your orientation.

Examples of Church orientation:

Worship Music

Preaching

Small Groups

Christian Education

Relationships

Growth

Children

Youth

Fill in the blank. As it is right now my church is
________________, orientated.

What is your church's message?

What is your church's medium?

What is your church's market?

What was the size of your congregation 2 years ago?

What was the size of your congregation 5 years ago?

What is the average age of your congregation?

Has your revenue increased, decreased or remained the same?

Are you closing the door to visitors? Example: Private jokes known only to the congregation can turn visitors away. Do you make it sound like you must have problems to become a member?

Values of your Church
Clarify the values of your church, values are a policing factor.
Select the three top important values in your church.

Example:

1. Personal relationships

2. Spiritual life

3. Authority of Scripture

After the top three, the rest are just what people want to hear.
List the things that are important in your church and score them in order of importance 1 to 10.

Example:

Growth - 3

Service - 8

Pastoral - 7

Evangelism -3

Events - 2

Social Work - 2

Facilities - 1

Finances - 4

Compare what you feel is important with the values you have selected for your church. Are you being truthful in what you say your values are and what you place importance on. For example if you place growth as a value and you are not growing, then growth is not a value.

In the example above, do you think that these are true values with the low importance placed on some of the items?

WHO NEEDS THE CHURCH?

Imagine a peasant in a remote part of the world who has never heard of Jesus Christ. This man tries to do his best for his family and be fair to others. When he dies, will he be denied eternal life with God?

Of course not!

The Bible itself says: "God is love, and whoever lives in love, lives in God, and God lives in him." 1 John 4:16

And so the bottom line for salvation is 'to live in love'. Mind you, this is no sugary sweet love, but rather a practical, self-giving service to one's brothers and sisters, and the acid test of true love is that it is inclusive - there can be no boundaries to our love, not even for enemies.

Love, mature selfless love, is the only criterion that signifies we have accepted God's gift of eternal life. If this is so, what need have we of Church, and all its accompanying dogma and ritual?

Jesus himself talks about going to our private place to be with God, and lambasts those who publicly parade their devotions.

A fundamental aspect of Christian theology is that all salvation is through Jesus. This means that Jesus' love-sacrifice on the cross, and the subsequent acceptance of that sacrifice by his heavenly Father, opens the gates of heaven to all humanity whether they know Jesus or not. Our peasant friend is redeemed by Jesus, because Jesus' love-sacrifice validates all human love as being the acceptance of God's gift of unconditional love, and although unworthy of God's life, that life is now given (past tense) to all who live in love.

Many folk who claim to be believers and followers of Jesus reject the Church, or at least try to get along without it. Many of these people, decent, sincere folk, have been hurt by the Church and cannot face the thought of returning.

Our peasant friend doesn't need the Church for him to be acceptable to God - why should we?

Has the Church then passed its 'soul-by-date'?

Of course not!

The Church was founded by Jesus, and founded for a purpose.

Jesus after all knew human nature only too well. No man is an island, and no community can stand without a structure.

Wherever two or more people meet in sincere and love-affirming fellowship, there is always something more than just their number. There is a power in the fellowship which means that 1 + 1 is always greater than 2. Jesus himself articulated this when he said: "wherever two or more are gathered in my name, I am there among them." Matthew 18:20

When Christians gather in sincere fellowship, Jesus is there! Guaranteed! We have his word for it.

Great, so let's all just meet in informal house groups and celebrate our mutual faith in Jesus! No need for special buildings, and certainly no need for huge multi-national religious organisations with their prescriptive dogmas and rules?

Cloud cuckoo land my friend... The early Church started out in such a way but with time and growing numbers, structures had to evolve. That's

just the way it is, and if we were somehow to stop and try to start again, the very same thing would happen. Indeed, many 'reformers' have tried over the centuries to rekindle the early days, but all they actually achieve is yet more fragmentation in the Church which is the body of Christ. And remember Jesus' earnest plea for unity? John 17:21

A Church without a structure would be like a body without a skeleton, and Jesus knows that, even if we don't. So we need a faith community, and not just for mutual support, but also for the continuance of the faith to following generations. I know Jesus today only because generations of forebears have carried the baton of faith across the centuries, sometimes at great personal cost. A 'private' spirituality may be very attractive, but ultimately it is selfish, and way short of what God is asking of us.

In a future article I hope to explain why I am and remain a Catholic, and to look at what the essentials of God's Church should be, but for this article suffice it to say that Jesus knew that his Church would need certain essentials if it was to last beyond the first flush of enthusiasm. It needed leadership and a teaching authority, and it needed the continual feeding with his word and the continual re-enacting of his ultimate self-

giving. We may baulk at these structures but that would be very short-sighted and foolish. That isn't to say that these structures and the Church itself need continual renewal and re-interpretation over time. Indeed, one of the great brakes on what the Holy Spirit wants to achieve is the human tendency to ossify the organic shoots of grace as time goes by.

What the Church needs throughout history is renewal, not reformation and certainly not schism. If we see aspects of church life that are unworthy of God's purpose, we need to work within the Church, not split off to start again, no matter how tempting that might be. On a personal level, it is not just what the Church can do for me - what can I do for the Church? One person, alive in the Holy Spirit, can work miracles of renewal.

A great friend and teacher once told me that his favourite image of the Church was the woman, hauled before Jesus, who had been caught in the very act of adultery. John 8: 11

The woman's guilt was very clear and the Jewish law was equally clear. She is an image of the Church, sinful beyond any doubt, and an expectant world waits to see her condemned by God. We know that Jesus did not condemn, and

instead told 'her' to go and be better. For Jesus loves his Church as a man loves his own body.

Ultimately, the Church is the servant of God's Kingdom, and the Church will pass away. Being human, it is riddled with sin, but it is also of God, and no evil will ever prevail against it.

It exists because humanly we need it to exist. God knows that even if we don't.

CHURCH HURTS - PAST AND PRESENT - FINDING RESOLUTIONS

Christians love one another, right? Well, that's the theory. Perhaps that's why church hurts sting more than most when they occur. Not only are relationships tearing at their heart, but there's the 'God factor' ripping through the divide.

Typical exasperated voices that traverse minds of hurt hearts:

1. "How could this happen to (or 'in') a church?"

2. "Why would they treat me this way?" says the exiting pastor, knowing no other trade (nor calling in life) than ministry, blindsided by a fickle church vote that ousts him/her.

3. "When did my pastor suddenly decide he/she doesn't like me?"

Pastors and church leaders are particularly susceptible to hurts - due their commitment and situations of congregants lacking appreciation - but they affect everyone who attends a place, and comes to a community, where trust is supposed to be easy; a 'given'. Those hurt find their trust

displaced for resentment that clings fast. Trust can't be manufactured.

When Church Hurts

The present-tense is handled first. How difficult is it to remain somewhere that's not welcoming? And the feeling of 'welcome' is a felt-thing. We feel welcome (and loved) or we don't.

Honesty and courage (honesty being a manifestation of courage) is vital. If honesty is not possible, for whatever reason, it makes situations intolerable. But how many tolerate the intolerable? Sometimes there's no fix other than to start afresh - so long as we're not continually church-shopping.

Being honest with a godly leadership is a way through, provided what goes with it is a mature approach to problem-solve. Transgressions (both ways) can be apologised for and forgiven. Ways forward can then be discussed.

Still, there are situations that are just plain difficult with no solution in sight.

Resolving Past Hurts - the Past

Churches are not just made up of Christians, but fallible, hurt-worthy human beings. Not only have people perhaps been hurt by churches and experiences with Christians, everyone has their share of brokenness that's brought to the table. Dealing with hurt adults is not unlike dealing with children. We're 'back there' in a flash.

'Sandpaper ministry' might sound like a character-building exercise, but when hurts are retained - and the temptation is always there - our experience of implicit trust goes south, and with it the intimacy of rapport.

Any time vacant thought about these experiences bridges minds it reinforces the damage. The deep though unvoiced emotion unfolds repetitively - thousands of times. A spiral of hurt attends. The trap is laid.

Awareness and Action

Making something of the hurt and doing something about it also requires honesty and courage - humility driving it. The only way out of these situations (when we're ready) is through a hard-nosed push to break clear. Admitting the hurt is an important first step (and if someone feels hurt, they're hurt).

Action is involving others. It's trusting trustworthy people to share with. Not tolerating the wrangling hurt one second longer than necessary; that's action.

But balanced with the action is gentility. Compassion is always the key; from those supporting, and for those hurt to be able to have the utmost compassion on themselves during the process.

CHURCH HURTS

Many fall foul of the religious system this side of the gates of eternity; and by 'religious system' I mean humankind's religious constructs and constraints that handcuff the ability for deity to break through and make a real spiritual difference in a believer's life. It happens in the world's religions and the root cause is selfish, unreconciled humanity.

A dangerous precedent is set when this occurs. People, and especially outsiders, begin to see the fingerprints and grip marks of humanity all over the spiritual--it crowds out any viable spirituality. It humanises what was never supposed to be.

Christianity is especially prone to this. This is probably because the concept of grace, as the key differentiation between Christianity and other world religions, is particularly sensitive to human disturbance. Worldly haranguing religious leaders, in their legalism, will smother the Spirit's gentle grace the moment they open their mouths and converse with people. It's apparent very early.

These leaders are the overwhelming minority. I mean, I don't actually know one of these--yet, they must exist by virtue of the stories we're told.

It needs to be said that:

Just because most confessing Christians can't or don't live truly after Jesus (as much as they can) isn't Jesus' fault. Some people blame Jesus or God (apparently these two entities are separate according to some) for how their lives have turned out or how Christians i.e. pastors 'have treated them.' But, these people forget very ⬛uickly; they've not dealt with God, but with fallible human beings.

Pastors are no more perfect than the next person, and the vast majority will ⬛uickly point that out themselves--in fact, their theology is proved correct when they do this. Sure, they must deal with many of their own moral issues and approach a higher standard to serve adequately in the church, but perfect people they will never be-- of all people, pastors know this. They know how imperfect humanity is. It is self-evident.

This takes us back to the hurt, disenfranchised person; "stung" by a church or by some negative or unloving experience of church.

Enter the inevitable paradoxes, the sweet at-times bitter ironies that confound the human being in his or her proud godless state:

Hurt people are amazingly consistent in their modus operandi--their own perception is they don't hurt; they get hurt. They have an acute sense of the external locus of control. It's the thing of, 'Stuff happens to me,' meaning they have a victim complex. To generalise and stereotype, they externalise everything and become responsible for nothing--not even that which would help their cause.

Another rampant sign of hurt people: aggression. Aggression equals fear. The aggressive personality is almost always the manifestation of an un-self-loved person deep down.

And at root--what is the source problem?

They've also not dealt with their own feelings of rejection. They've not sought God's unconditional acceptance to ameliorate their own sense of unacceptance. Yes, the very people who reject Christ and his church are shrieking in the fear deep down--and Jesus is the only One who can save them!

What a mess! There are many unfortunates. The only thing we can pray for is the people least likely to surrender, will.

And this attends to something all people must account for: rejection and acceptance. There is nothing more profound to human experience than this. No matter how well loved we were as children, we have all felt--and are all plagued by, to varying degrees--sweeping rejection.

The unfortunates who can never constrain their fear long enough to see and admit this will crash into a Christless eternity, and that collision course beckons, even now.

The truth is we'll always feel rejectable until we've genuinely felt the loving embrace of Christ--the One who never condemns, because grace can never condemn.

In Summary

There are genuine cases of people being hurt by churches. The perpetrators could not possibly know Christ, and I'd posit that they'd not dealt with their rejection, experienced Christ's cross or swam in his unconditionally accepting grace.

Love cannot hurt. Neither can grace. But hurt people hurt people--whether these are inept ministers or the hurt people themselves. Yes, many times the people hurt in church simply haven't dealt with their own sense of clinging

rejection; they've not truly been introduced to the abiding grace of unconditional acceptance.

HEALING THE HURT - WHAT YOU CAN DO TO HELP

Everyone feels it and some people can get over it faster than others. Get over what? Hurt. Hurt comes in many forms. Simply living life, you will surely meet a situation or circumstance that hurts. Nothing physical, just that feeling in which you need to talk about it, but no one seems to understand on listed without passing harsh insensitive judgement. Feelings of sadness and loneliness are magnified when no one seems to understand not do they what to listen. Just because you may take a bit longer that most to get over something, it doesn't mean you are weak.

I firmly believe the following, as believers we should be ready to help anyone whom we see, needing a kind word or a listening ear. You don't have to go far to find or meet someone who is hurting. While it's true, many people will reject your help, there is always someone who will accept and appreciate it.

Compassion is something you don't hear much about in the Church. Church members of this modern time seem more preoccupied with the perception of their spirituality and they overlook those around them. Businesses, churches and

families were devastated by the spiral down of the economy. There are so may opportunities to minister to and encourage people, I often wonder, where are the church members? Where are the missionaries?

People are hurting and I have come to learn that people will seek someone who will just listen or show they care. When you are sitting in the break room at your job and someone who never has conversation with you, begins to talk, listen to them. At some point in the conversation, they will share something that is or has hurt them. If church members would allow the Spirit of God to lead and guide them, they will be able to meet the needs of the hurting people around them.

Helping

Everyday, ordinary people are going outside of their comfort zones to say a kind and encouraging word to someone. Smiling is so contagious, if you smile and say hello to someone who is not smiling, often times they will smile back at you. When someone begins to share something personal, don't start telling them about the love of God and how Jesus heals. Hear me out, sometimes it good to just listen and wait for the opportunity to share Christ. You can show the love of Jesus Christ by simply caring.

Listening

Who has the time for it? It's obvious to the person, who feels they can share something personal with you, that you have the time. Having the experience of walking down the hall at work one day, I had no Idea of the story my facial expression told in the early morning hours. A concerned co-worker, stopped me and asked me, "Nate, are you okay?" The fact that someone showed concerned, was moving.

Compassion still exists among people today. We all share the same planet, breathing the same air and drinking the same water. Don't let compassion be something only read about in periodicals or history books. Be compassionate, care about your fellow-man.

SEXUAL ABUSE OF YOUTH WITHIN THE CHURCH - STEPS TOWARD RECOVERY

I can tell you from many discussions with people young and old that sexual abuse in the church is more common than mentioned. According to The Abel and Harlow Child Molestation Prevention Study, 93% of admitted Child Molesters claimed to be religious (Abel, G.G., & Harlow, N (2001). Even though we know that sexual abuse occurs with those who do not claim Christianity, the number of those claiming religion is extremely high. Many people claim to know what the bible says about sexual sin. However, when a sexual sin is broken by the one who preaches it; the media uses it as an avenue to find fault within the religious community. Satan uses this to destroy people's belief in God.

The goals of this eBook are to:

1. Show youth and adults how to heal and overcome sexual abuse within the church.

2. Equip parents and adults in the Christian faith on how to minister to those who have been sexually abused in the church.

Once these goals are completed within this article, Satan can no longer have victory over the victims life. We know that sexual abuse among youth in the church is only a spirit that has been released in the earth in order to hinder the body of Christ at large. However, through prayer, trust in God, and trust in his word we cannot lose.

Sexual Abuse among children has always been an issue in society; however, it has become an increasing problem that has caused much physical, mental and emotional damage. Because of the increase of sexual abuse among youth, more and more people are finding ways to help youth who have been sexually abused.

Sexual Abuse among the youth doesn't care about age, race, religion, or financial status. It is one of the tools Satan uses in order to try to destroy our youth. Psalms 8: 2 says, "Nursing infants gurgle choruses about you; toddlers shout the songs that drown out enemy talk, and silence atheist babble." (The Message Version) Satan uses sexual abuse among youth in and outside the church in order to sow seeds that would destroy their destiny. He wants to silence the mouth of our youth forever. However, if one will trust in God, his purposes will always prevail!

Sexual immorality is an ever increasing issue not only in the world but in the church as well. Because of this increasing issue, sexual immorality has now even spilled over and is affecting the children in the body of Christ. We as members of the body of Christ have the responsibility to allow God to use us in becoming a solution to the ever growing problem through prayer and support.

Today, many churches try to keep sexual immorality hidden inside the house of God. We must recognize that God ultimately sees everything. He will bring to light those things that have been practiced in darkness. Fornication, adultery, homosexuality and molestation exist in many churches across the world. The body of Christ has a responsibility to make sure that none of these sins be named among us. The places where the body of Christ goes to worship should represent God's presence and his holiness.

If there is a deep hurt within your heart and you don't know how to let it go, then I'm here to tell you that God is a deliverer right now! Have you been sexually abused in the church by someone you trusted and it has leaded you down a road of promiscuity? Maybe you have been sexually abused by someone outside the church that you trusted. If so, then I want to pray this prayer with

you because God is real and he is a deliverer! I know him to be a deliverer from my own experiences. God has brought me through the hurt, the pain, the rejection, the disappointment and has set me free. Now it is your turn to be free!

True healing from any hurt has to come from God's word. Hebrews 4:12 says "For the word of God is quick, and powerful, and sharper than any two-edged sword, piercing even to the dividing asunder of soul and spirit, and of the joints and marrow, and is a discerner of the thoughts and intents of the heart." God loves us enough to search deep within our inner being to bring healing.

We have the option to go to counseling and to talk to others. However, until we choose to let go and allow the word of God to penetrate deep within our spirits, we will never experience true healing through God's word. Trusting in God's word to heal us is a choice. God's word is here to heal us and deliver us from the hurt of abuse. But until we open our hearts to receive the deliverance, healing for us will remain dormant. We must realize that if we choose not to receive the deliverance of God's word in our heart, it still does not make God's word of none effect. God's word will always have power to deliver us whether we choose to let it or not. Some people would rather remain in

past hurts. They will allow others to enable their hurt instead of receiving their healing. Those who truly want to be set free will seek God's word for deliverance. We are creature of choice. God will not force his deliverance upon us. We have to make the decision to receive his healing.

God also sends others to help those through the sexual abuse. At many stages in life, God sends and ordains anointed mentors in order to take you from one stage in life to another. Having an anointed mentor plays an important part when it comes to complete healing and deliverance from the scars of abuse in the church.

There are several things to remember concerning youth who have been sexually abused. It is important to understand that sometimes children are afraid to tell others due to guilt and fear. Parents and youth leaders have to know how to communicate with your child. Don't overreact if a child discloses the abuse. Pastors ask for references when getting youth volunteers and prayerfully choose God fearing leaders. Finally, train staff on how to work with youth.

In closing, understand that the abuser is almost always a person who has been abused himself. So, if you are an abuser, the first thing to do is to forgive yourself. You then need to release those

who have abused you and this can be done through counseling. Get Help. It is never too late to start!